# Affiliate Marketing

## The Ultimate Beginners Guide to Learn How to start an online Business

## Selling Other People's Products to Make Passive Income

# Table of Contents

**Targeting Your Audience**

1. International usage of mobile devices

2. The shift in human behavior that is occurring because of smartphones and other mobile devices

**Most Important Differences between Mobile and Desktop Marketing**

- Types of traffic

- Understanding intent and its role in the price of traffic

- Important traffic parameters to pay attention to

- Learning curve

- User intent

- Targeting power

- Scalability

- Relative costs

- Mobile friendliness

- Making different types of traffic work

# What is Affiliate Marketing and Who Is It For?

Affiliate marketing is a type of marketing in which an organization rewards its affiliates for bringing in customers or visitors through the affiliates' marketing efforts conducted independently of the organization itself.

Most businesses in the world want to grow and increase their revenues by getting more customers. There are several ways how they can accomplish this. The first way is to find customers willing to pay for the products or services that these businesses are selling. They can spend a fortune on advertising, or they can get someone else to get customers for them.

Let's say a business is willing to pay $40 for every sale. This means that it can either spend money on marketing or pay it to its affiliates via commissions.

Affiliate marketing can be one of the quickest ways to make money on the Internet. To get started with affiliate marketing, you do not need a website, a list of customers or a product. You can simply get an affiliate link, start promoting it and start making cash immediately.

Most of the biggest merchants on the Internet, including Amazon, do have affiliate programs. This means that using affiliate marketing you can participate in the sales of some of the hottest products on the Internet even though it is someone else who has created those products.

Affiliate marketing is also a great way to get started with marketing on the Internet. A lot of people don't try selling something online because they erroneously believe that they need to create a product or a service first. However, this is simply not true. You do not have to create anything. You can simply do some research, find out what sells well and start selling and advertising it, too. This way you do not have to spend countless hours creating or sourcing products but can start making money and learning Internet marketing by doing very quickly.

Finally, affiliate marketing is a great way to add streams of income to already existing businesses. If you have a business, the fact that your customers are buying from you means that they trust you and that they value what you have. You have a relationship with your customers that you can expand using affiliate marketing, recommend products or services and make money in the meantime.

For example, if you sell information products to a certain business niche about becoming more successful by making marketing measurable, you can become an affiliate and start selling software that helps your clients accomplish their goals. You could also sell them products and services that help them run their businesses. If you also teach personal productivity, you could be selling vitamins and supplements. The list of the things that you could do is virtually unlimited.

One of the biggest misconceptions about affiliate marketing is that it doesn't take any work. Affiliate business model makes perfect sense to businesses that want to recruit affiliates to sell their products or services. Such businesses don't have to invest in advertising or worry about spending advertising dollars ineffectively. All the risk in this business model falls on the shoulders of the affiliates.

As an affiliate, you do not receive a guaranteed percentage of the profits. Your income in not assured. The profit that you make depends entirely on making sales or delivering leads for an amount that is less than the commission that you receive.

If you are getting $40 per sale, you will make $10 per transaction if it costs you $30 to get a customer. If it costs you $60 to get a customer, you will lose $20 per transaction.

At this point, you may be wondering why someone would choose to become an affiliate. There are many reasons why affiliate marketing works for both product creators and affiliates. One of the most important reasons why affiliates choose to do what they do is freedom, flexibility, and choice.

Creation of a product can take a lot of time, money and resources and a product can turn out to be a complete flop. Customers may think that the product is overpriced or that the products from competitors have better features or durability.

In either scenario, the company will get into serious trouble because its survival depends on the sales of the product.

If you are an affiliate, in most cases you couldn't care less about the product. If you discover that a product doesn't sell well, you can start promoting a new product in a few hours.

This flexibility means that you can switch between different niches and always find something that's new, exciting and wanted by the customers. It may be a weight loss pill, an information product that helps singles get better dates or a new app from a creator in Silicon Valley.

Skilled affiliates are always in demand because there are and always will be successful businesses looking to pay to get more new customers.

As an affiliate, you never have to worry about creating new products. All you need to be able to do is find the next great product or service and get your commission when you sell it. This means that as an affiliate you have an opportunity to get a piece of the pie from almost any great product or service in the world.

# Three Ways To Structure Affiliate Agreements

Practically speaking, there are three ways for affiliates to get their money. The first way is

**Pay Per Sale**

This is the simplest affiliate marketing payment model. In this model, you get a fixed amount of money for every sale that you make. In the previous example, an affiliate was getting a PPS rate of $40 for every sale.

Getting paid per sale has an upside of affiliates receiving the highest possible one-time payments. The problem with this model of payment is that the cost of information that you need to have as an affiliate to decide whether you want to sell a high-priced product goes up exponentially with the end price of the product.

For example, let's say that a business is willing to pay you $200 per sale. In order to be able to tell whether you advertising campaigns are successful or not, you would most likely need to spend much more than $200.

**Pay Per Lead**

A lead is a person that a merchant can follow up with. For example, a business may be selling software. The first step in the sales process is a presentation of the software to an interested party. The interested party, in this case, is a lead. Every affiliate pay per lead campaign will have its own definition of a lead. In some cases, a lead can be something as simple as an email address. In other cases, a lead would mean a person who fills out a four-page survey without skipping any questions.

The merchant would then typically calculate how many leads it needs to make a sale. For example, if a merchant is willing to pay $40 on every sale and the merchant needs twenty leads to make one sale, it would usually pay $2 per lead.

One of the reasons why so many affiliates prefer the pay per lead model to the pay per sale model is that it provides them with a lot of data points for the same cost.

If it takes you $30 to make a sale, you will need to spend $90 to make three sales. Three sales is not a lot of information, and you can't draw a lot of conclusions from this information.

At the same time, if you are getting leads for $1, spending $90 means that you'll get ninety leads. This will provide you with many more dots on the graph and much more information to take a look at and draw conclusions from.

For example, you can split-test several landing pages from the very beginning and find out that Landing Page A brought in forty leads while Landing Page B brought only five.

The pay per lead model is also the most forgiving to beginners. It is much easier to get just an email address from someone than to have them fill out a multiple-page questionnaire or place an order. However, this doesn't mean you can deliver leads of bad quality. If you are getting paid based on the number of leads that you deliver, it is still critically important that the merchant that you are working with gets the sales at the ratio that he or she expects.

**Revenue Share**

Revenue share is the third and last model of payment in affiliate marketing. Just like its name suggests, this model is an arrangement between an affiliate and a merchant in which the affiliate is being paid based on the revenue that the merchant gets from the customers that the affiliate brings in.

This model doesn't have a lot of pitfalls of PPL and PPS models, but it has its own issues. With profit sharing comes risk sharing.

A merchant may be getting the bulk of the profits from the repeat purchases. This means that as an affiliate you may have to wait several months to get the same financial returns that you will get from a PPS or a PPL deal.

A revenue share agreement makes perfect sense for an affiliate if you know that as an affiliate you will be able to bring in customers that will be responsible for the majority of sales in the long run. For example, imagine a customer who spends $20 on the first transaction and $50,000 in the first year.

If you are being paid based on a PPL or PPS model, you will probably get around thirty percent of $20. However, if you have a revenue share agreement, you will get 30% of $50,000 deposited to your bank account.

# How Affiliates Make Their Money

The goal of any business venture, including your activities as an affiliate, is to make money and maximize profits.

As an affiliate, you have two main ways to make money on the front-end. These ways are

1.    Selling products or services to more people and

2.    Increasing the conversion rates for every step of your affiliate process. The conversion rate is the percentage of people who take the desired action, be in leaving an email address,

completing a survey or buying a product or service.

Conversion rate plays a critically important role in affiliate marketing. For example, if you bring in one hundred leads a day to a sales page and 2% of them buy, you will get paid for two purchases. If you can bring the same number of visitors, but increase the conversion rate from 2% to 5%, you will get paid for five purchases, which is 250% more money from the same number of visitors.

No matter how you bring traffic, it will cost you money, time or both. This is why you want to take advantage of the third way of making money as an affiliate, which is building your own list.

If you rank your page or website high in the search engines, build a community and a relationship with your customers, you will be able to make money even if your current merchant goes out of business or decides to pull the offer that you got started with. You'll simply be able to replace one offer with something else and continue to make money from your list.

## How to find profitable niches

If you look at a website like Amazon or some of the most popular tools to find affiliate offers, you will find tens if not hundreds of products and offers that you can promote. Some merchants specialize in just one niche, such as games, apps, adult entertainment, weight loss, dating and so one, while other merchants have all kinds of products and services at the same time.

This is why no matter what path you decide to take in affiliate marketing, you will have more offers available to you than you could possibly promote in ten lifetimes.

It is good to be open to new ideas, but you at a certain point you will need to focus. One of the ways to do that is to deal with one niche, learn about that niche and make your money in it.

For example, if you decide to focus on the weight loss market, you are going to ignore all the offers in the dating, skincare, and other verticals. You also can't be interested in gaming or financial instruments at the same time. This will reduce the amount of offers that you will have available to several hundred. Out of those, there are probably ten to twenty offers that you can promote and make a profit. Out of these ten to twenty, there are most likely two to three that you can scale to make you a thousand dollars a day or more.

This is why determination, focus, and specialization are so important. It is simply impossible to keep a focus on several niches and all the offers that they have. You need to become a market specialist and learn everything there is to learn about a market.

To become successful in affiliate marketing, you need to become much more productive than the majority of other affiliates in that market. The only way to do that is to add more value to the sales process. To do that you will have to learn about your strengths or build them from scratch if you think that you don't have any.

Affiliate marketing is similar to market trading in that those who don't know what they are doing are making no money. The industry may look attractive, but becoming successful in it does require work. If someone is making money in skincare, it doesn't mean that you will also make money in skincare. What it means is that this affiliate knows what he or she is doing. It is more about individual strengths, strategies, and planning than it is about a niche.

It is very helpful to choose a vertical that you are passionate and interested about. If you just go into a niche because you think it's profitable, you will soon discover that there are a lot of other affiliates who have a better understanding of the market and the products than you do. Such affiliates will make progress while you will keep getting distracted by other opportunities because you have no real interest in the niche.

The good news is that affiliate marketing has all kinds of niches and anyone can find something that they are interested in, something that suits their personality and their strength.

Below you will find an overview of such niches.

Heath, Self, and Wealth are the three most universal markets. They have products and services that you can promote to multiple types of customers. These markets are based on the most fundamental human needs, wants and desires. You probably see your friends discussing diets and posting selfies from the gym on Instagram all the time. Your other friends care a lot about making more money, becoming more financially stable and making better financial decisions.

This is why one of the surefire ways to becoming a successful affiliate is to pick a mass market, get in on a growing trend, find a product with the most compelling promise and sell this product.

**Health**

The same is true of the health vertical. No market attracts as much attention and scrutiny as health niche does. This market contains a number of products, including diet plans, weight loss pills, weight loss food programs and detox food and drinks and other products attached to health promises.

Some of the most popular affiliate offers of the past and the present have been vanity-driven. This market is so huge because health often has a direct impact on appearance and people would pay a lot to stop feeling depressed or ashamed about their looks.

Another reason why affiliate health market is so big is that the available information about health is very contradictory. The concept of immediate gratification plays an important role in it, too. Most people want the results without doing all the hard work. They want a product, a bottle full of pills that will do all the work for them. Affiliate marketers in the dieting vertical have learned to use this fact to make massive amounts of money.

**Self**

Various products that have to deal with the human desire for self-improvement are a multi-billion dollar industry.

Self-improvement can take all kinds of forms and shapes, from learning a language to advancing a career to improving the quality of life. People often pay significant amounts of money to feel better about themselves and their lives, to get ahead and develop new skills and habits.

If you want to learn more about the self vertical, you should start with familiarizing yourself with the Hierarchy of Needs by Abraham Maslow. Maslow presents human needs in the form of a pyramid.

At the bottom of the pyramid are physiological needs of human beings, such as food, water, sleep, breathing, excretion. From a marketing standpoint, hardly anyone needs a product about how to breathe. However, even the needs for food, sex, excretion and sleep already present a lot of opportunities for marketers.

The most important idea of the Maslow's hierarchy of needs is that the higher up the pyramid you go, the greater the focus on self and on the needs such as actualization, morality, spontaneity and so on.

Self-actualization is located at the very top of the pyramid. Self-actualization is a desire of a human being to be the best version of him- or herself.

Most affiliate products belong to the esteem layer of the Maslow's pyramid. This layer has needs such as self-esteem, confidence, achievement, respect of and by others. Examples of products that fall into this layer are products about how to quit smoking, how to get a better job, how to become more self-confident, how to influence people, become more attractive to the opposite sex and so on.

Two of the most popular self niches are wealth and dating. They are so popular because they solve the problems that most of the people face at some point in their lives.

The wealth category mostly appeals to the human emotion of greed and wanting to have more. It has a number subcategories that target one or more of the following: people who are in debt, people who feel stuck and/or underpaid at their current job or are afraid that they will lose their jobs, people that are drawn by materialistic desires and crave the social status that comes together with being paid more than the peers.

There are two main kinds of offers that you will see in the wealth category. The first one positions ordinary opportunities as having hidden powers, for example, "Get insanely rich with 5 cent Facebook ads." The second one promotes getting an edge in an industry where customers know it is possible to make money. Examples of such industries are real estate and FOREX trading.

The first category caters to mass markets and is, therefore, more scalable. The second category requires more trust and specialized knowledge. In return, you can expect higher margins and considerably higher price points.

For example, certain financial newsletters sell for hundreds of dollars in monthly fees, and the affiliate commissions are proportionately large. This happens because the products demand a certain caliber of the customer. It costs money to find these customers, but such customers are willing to pay for quality products created just for them.

For an affiliate in the wealth category, this means that you need to be choosing your products very wisely and know what you are doing. You can either go with cheap, generic products created for mass markets, or you can promote big-ticket items selling which is a lot of work that comes with much nicer margins.

**Dating**

Dating is a subcategory of the self market. We are talking about it separately because it is one of the most popular and biggest niches for affiliate marketers. The typical customer for the products in the dating niche is male and young, either in his twenties or thirties. Products for older folks do exist, but the markets tend to be smaller.

One of the popular affiliate agreements requires an affiliate to bring in leads that will create their personal profiles on online dating websites.

There are two main ways of getting paid in this scenario. In the first one, you get paid when someone creates a profile. In the second one, you get paid when your lead creates a profile and confirms the email address.

One of the biggest challenges of doing business in the dating vertical is to be able to deliver paying customers to the merchants. The amount of free information and services in the niche is extremely large and making people pay for something can be very hard.

**Insurance**

Promotions of the insurance offers can be very lucrative, but it is definitely not for newbies. To get paid for promoting insurance offers, you will most likely need to match prospects and insurance quotes for home insurance, car insurance, life insurance and so on.

This field can be extremely profitable because many insurance companies offer very generous commissions on leads. The problem with this field is that insurance companies themselves use advanced demographic targeting and are spending very heavily on Google AdWords and Facebook ads. This means that Google Adwords costs are often over $20 per click and even more. Obviously, as a small affiliate, you can't compete with such prices and spends.

**Finance**

Finance vertical is probably even tougher to crack for affiliate marketers than the insurance market. Finance includes credit card, mortgage and loan offers and quotes. Just like with insurance, the best moment to capture a prospect is when the prospect is actively looking for a product or a service. For this reason, financial companies are spending very heavily on Google AdWords and most likely you won't be able to compete with them.

## Gaming

You will find a lot of games and apps that pay for sign-ups, installations or first plays. The fast development of the market of mobile devices has created big opportunities for this market. Gaming has a great appeal for all kinds of people and companies like Zynga have proven it. They have built addiction into their games and took it to a whole new level, a level that includes demographics of senior citizens and stay-at-home moms. Similarly to other categories, affiliates who really succeed with gaming offers are usually specialists. They learn their market and its wants and desires inside out and then create ads that appeal to these wants and desires both intellectually and emotionally. Great affiliates usually have a passion for games or even just certain genres of games. This helps them figure out the trends of the industry and be able to spot games that become huge successes.

**What else is there?**

We have just looked at some of the most popular categories of offers in affiliate marketing. What we've missed is the

Everything Else category, which is probably as big, if not bigger, as everything that we have already mentioned.

The truth is that you can find an affiliate program for almost anything that can benefit from getting leads online. For example, you can stick to a small local market, dominate the market and be selling leads to local lawyers, dentists, plastic surgeons, car repair shops and so on.

# Targeting Your Audience

Once you decide on the niche and the products that you will be promoting as an affiliate, you need to figure out what devices you will be targeting.

Different demographics use different devices, which is why it is so important to first choose your niche, category and offers that you will be working with.

There are three main types of devices. They are desktops (even though it is called desktop, this category includes all computers, both PCs and Macs, laptops and desktops), mobile devices (Androids and iOS) and tablets such as iPads, Kindles and so on.

If you choose to target only desktops, you will miss out on a significant percentage of the market. According to the information released by analytics company StatCounter, total Internet usage on mobile devices has exceeded total usage on desktop devices for the first time in October of 2016. StatCounter provided data that showed mobile devices being responsible for 51.3% of the worldwide Internet traffic and desktops getting 48.7%.

This being said, targeting desktops only is still a viable option. This market has been lucrative for many years and will continue to bring a lot of profits to affiliate marketers despite the gradual shift towards mobile devices.

Many affiliates place tablet users in the same category as desktop users. Many affiliate merchants also have the same terms and conditions for tablet and desktop users. This means that your payouts will also be the same. However, the conversion rate can vary considerably depending on the device.

You will see some tablet-only campaigns fail miserably while others will deliver incredible ROI. Many affiliates do not bother to target their advertising campaigns by tablet only. This creates a void in the market and the bids for tablet clicks can be considerably cheaper compared to desktop and smartphone clicks. However, these clicks may not convert into buyers or leads, which is why testing is so important.

Finally, you can target users of mobile devices such as smartphones. As we mentioned earlier, this is a big deal, and it will only be getting bigger in the future.

There are two reasons why targeting mobile devices has a huge potential.

## 1. International usage of mobile devices

In many developing countries people do not have computers. Their first and only device through which that can have access to the Internet is their mobile phone.

This may not seem like a big deal to you if you grew up in the West and had a computer since you were in middle school. Most people in the developing countries couldn't afford a

computer in the past and can't afford a

computer today. However, the prices for mobile devices keep falling and this means that cheap mobile phones connect a lot of people to the Internet for the first time. These people didn't have access to the Internet before, but they do now thanks to inexpensive mobile devices.

What is also important to understand is that people in the West are bombarded with marketing messages day and night. For this reason, conversions in the Western countries are often much lower compared to the developing countries. People in the United States, Canada, Europe and Australia are used to seeing a lot of advertising. They've grown numb to it. To people in the developing countries, advertising can be new and exciting. It is still something that they pay attention to.

This can be compared to the first years when email became available to the public. People were excited to get emails. They were waiting for someone to send them an email. They opened all emails that they got. Obviously, this is very different from what is happening today when most of the electronic mailboxes in the West are full of unread messages and people view email as a chore. However, in many of the developing countries email, Internet advertising and marketing are still new and exciting.

## 2 The shift in human behavior that is occurring because of smartphones and other mobile devices

Before smartphones, people did not realize all the opportunities that came with having the Internet in their pockets. Today many people are convinced that having Internet on-the-go is something they absolutely need. They are used to shopping on their mobile devices. They play games while waiting in line or riding the subway. Their lives depend more and more on having instant access to the Internet. In 2015 a Qualcomm survey reported that 29% of Americans looked at their smartphones immediately after they woke up and right before they went to bed. 29% is about one-third of the population. At the same time, 37% of the population say that they check their mobile devices at least every thirty minutes during the day. These results are both tragic and exciting. If you just glance around you when you are in the office, when you are walking down the street or are commuting to work, you will see that most people are sucked into their mobile devices. They don't really see what's going

around them. They are only paying attention to

their phones.

This trend is irreversible. Our society will never

go back to checking email once a day on a

desktop computer.

Having a smartphone at all times is also

leading to some other profound changes. Our

attention spans are getting shorter and shorter.

People are becoming more reachable than ever.

If in the past the only way to get to someone

was a TV commercial, today smartphones,

smart TVs and other devices offer an array of

methods to deliver a message.

# Most Important Differences between Mobile and Desktop Marketing

Advertising on mobile phones is very different from advertising on desktops. The good news for you if you are a newbie is that you can learn mobile marketing the right way from the very beginning. You do not have to unlearn years or even decades of bad habits.

The biggest difference between desktop and mobile advertising is that mobile users are much more attached to their devices both literally and figuratively.

The problem with mobile advertising is that specifications of mobile phones are much less predictable than those of desktop PCs. When you create a new web campaign, all you have to worry about is a few antiquated browsers and a few fonts that your target audience may have an issue with.

There are many more problems that you will have to face if you decide to advertise on mobile devices. This happens because mobile devices come in a variety of sizes and can have a number of operational systems, fonts, and browsers.

Here are just a few things that you will need to consider:

Screen size. How do your landing page and your offers look on various devices, from the

cheapest smartphone to the most expensive
iPad Pro?

Connection type. Are your targets browsing the
Internet via really fast wi-fi from home or are
they doing so via a slow and expensive mobile
carrier? How will this affect the loading time of
pages and download speeds?

Features of the devices. What features does the
device have or not have? How will they affect
what you are trying to accomplish?

Operating system. Are most of your visitors
using Apple devices? Android devices?
Something else?

If you combine the factors that we just outlined, you will see that they are literally thousands of different possible combinations when it comes to models, operational systems, screen sizes, carriers, brands and so on.

What you need to understand the mobile landscape is that it is fragmented in such a manner that only certain combinations will generate profits.

If you are only advertising on desktops, you should be concerned with landing pages, ads, banners, placements, and targeting.

If you are advertising on mobile, you need to get all these elements right and make sure that you know how to deal with limitations of the technologies that your targets use to access the Internet.

**Types of traffic**

Essentially, there are two kinds of traffic that you can drive to your offers. They are free and paid. While generating free traffic could make you money, it usually takes much more time to generate free traffic than it does to drive paid traffic to a page.

Because of this, it is usually much harder to scale free traffic. This is why if you eventually want to make a lot of money in affiliate marketing, you need to learn paid traffic.

From a beginner perspective, free traffic may look very attractive. Learning search engine optimization, posting in the forums and

Facebook groups require no financial investment and make affiliate marketing look risk-free. However, even if you are not investing any money, you are investing your time, which is the most precious thing that you have. The biggest risk that you are taking in any venture is that you may wake up one day and realize that you have spent a lot of time, yet did not accomplish your goals.

Focusing on a venture where you won't need to spend any money may sound like a nice safety net, but in reality, it also ties you to a limiting mindset that will prevent you from achieving major success in the long term.

The key to unlocking exponential growth in affiliate marketing is being able to spend money and scale campaigns while saving time. You simply can't make a lot of money if it takes you several months to rank a website and then you are 100% visible to your competition because you are on the first page of Google. Add to this the fact that your success is completely dependent on Google's ranking algorithm, and you'll realize why making money with free traffic is not a surefire way to success in affiliate marketing.

The only alternative to paid traffic that exists is the viral promotion model. In this model you don't pay for advertising and your product basically sells itself.

Most of the offers that you will be promoting as an affiliate are not viral offers. If they were viral, the merchant wouldn't need you. This is why trying to make affiliate offers to go viral is usually painful and unlikely.

With paid advertising, you can not only build campaigns quickly, but you can also test a lot of landing pages, offers, and funnels in a short period of time. You don't have to worry about search engines crawling and ranking your pages. You can do whatever you want at whatever speed you choose in order to accomplish your goals.

If you figure out how to create a positive ROI, you can start scaling your campaigns and the sky is the limit.

**Understanding intent and its role in the price of traffic**

When you are buying traffic, intent is one of the factors that will have an influence on how much you will pay for the traffic.

For example, if a user types into Google "where do I buy home insurance in zip code 33137?" – that's a very serious statement of intent to buy. It is very clear from this search query that the user is a potential customer looking to spend money.

The stage before this one is the research stage. When someone decides that they want to buy, but they are not sure what they will be buying, they type into Google things like "home insurance reviews," "types of home insurance," "which home insurance is right for me" and so on.

The problem is that you would rarely be able to buy traffic that consists of people ready to buy right now. The cost-per-click numbers for such searches are extremely high, and a lot of businesses are bidding on them themselves.

You job as an affiliate is not going to be this simple. However, Google AdWords and Facebook are newbie-friendly in the sense that it is possible to use them to find people who are ready to be sold to even though they may not be actively looking or ready to buy in the moment.

The difference between advertising on Google and on Facebook is that on Google people are actively looking for information. On Facebook, you would usually enter someone's newsfeed without the person actively looking for you or information from you.

This means that you need to approach advertising on Facebook differently. Instead of relying on keywords that show buying intent you need to use demographic targeting to find users based on the information that Facebook has about them, such as their interests, age, marital status, occupation, level of income and so on.

When promoting an offer on Facebook, you must first think about who is the person that is going to respond to the offer. The more you know, the better. For example, if you know that your offer is going to sound really compelling to men ages 35 to 45 with a military background who are also regular church-goers, you can use Facebook to create an audience that consists only of the demographic described above and then you can be promoting your offer only to this audience.

**Important traffic parameters to pay attention to**

For each type of traffic that you will be considering for you offers you need to look at the following factors:

**Learning curve**

How much experience do you have with this kind of traffic? How much experience do you have with this target audience? It goes without saying that you want the learning curve to be as small as possible. You simply can't make money if you need to spend months studying various markets before you are able to run profitable campaigns. As we talked before, this is the reason why you want to specialize and learn some segments of the market really well.

**User intent**

How much selling will you have to do in order to accomplish the objectives that you want to accomplish? Is the target market performing the desired actions already for some other products or services? Who else is selling to them and what are they doing?

For example, if your goal is to generate leads from a market that thinks that all information marketing products are a scam, you may have a tough road ahead of you. It is much easier to accomplish the same task while working with the market that is already spending money on information products. This is why it is so important to analyze user intent and know your targets.

**Targeting power**

How quickly and easily can you get to the audience? Can you target it really well? If you can't, chances are that the conversion rates for your ads are going to be really small and Facebook, Google or a different advertising platform will decide that your ads are not relevant. What happens next is your price per click usually goes up significantly because that's how Google and Facebook make sure that their advertisers create ads that do not annoy the users. If you can't target your audience effectively, you most likely will not be able to make your campaigns work.

## Scalability

Let's assume that you are able to get a positive return on investment for a campaign that you are running. How hard will it be for you to scale that campaign? Ideally, you want the kinds of traffic where you can 2x, 5x or 10x the amount of traffic just with a few clicks of a mouse. If increasing the traffic by ten or twenty percent means that you have to spend significant amounts of time creating new campaigns, you will not be able to make a lot of money. This is something we talked about before in this book. One of the keys to success in affiliate marketing is to be able to scale what works quickly and easily.

**Relative costs**

How cheap or expensive is the traffic? What budget do you need to test your campaigns? It goes without saying that you always want to minimize your risks and you never want to test something you are not sure about if you have to spend a huge amount of money.

**Mobile friendliness**

Does the traffic have the potential to convert well on mobile or does it consist primarily of desktop users?

**Making different types of traffic work**

In this part of the book, we will take a look at different types of traffic and discuss their pros and cons.

**Paid search**

Paid search includes engines such as Google, Yahoo, and Bing. It is one of the fastest ways to drive high-quality traffic to your pages.

Paid search has advertisers that spend a lot of money and are willing to pay significant sums for every single click. Also, Google considers affiliates to be less desirable advertisers compared to big corporations or small businesses. This means that you will need to work really hard and make sure that you do not look like a spammy affiliate. If Google doesn't like what you are offering, you are likely to find your Google AdWords account suspended.

The learning curve of using paid search advertising is somewhat simple. You can get started very quickly by choosing your keywords, creating ads and tracking the results. Costs are going to be easy to see and measure.

At the same time, Google AdWords and Google Analytics have a lot of features that may take a lot of time to learn and implement. The good news is that you don't need a lot of those features to get started.

Assuming that you've chosen great keywords, you will not be able to match traffic to offers better than on Google and other search engines. Google traffic is also extremely scalable. At the same time, Bing and Yahoo have very small amounts of traffic compared to Google.

The problem with Google is that you will not be able to find obvious keywords with buying intent that are profitable. Google AdWords has a lot of players in it, and costs per click can be very high depending on the market.

**Search Engine Optimization**

It seems that today most of the people who are selling something on the Internet, be it gigantic corporations or small businesses, are talking about search engine optimization or SEO. The reason why SEO is so popular is very simple: it's free. If you optimize your website properly, if you get inbound links and if you don't have the money to spend on advertising, you can work really hard and have your pages appear on the first page of Google for some very lucrative keywords.

However, in a lot of cases SEO is similar to gambling, because Google may change its algorithms or introduce new updates at any time, which is something it is doing on a regular basis. That's when you can easily go from page one to page twenty in a few hours. If SEO is the only thing you are doing to bring in traffic, you are gambling.

The learning curve for SEO isn't very hard, but SEO is a lot of hard, manual work. While you can target specific demographics or specific keywords, you are always at Google's mercy and what you are doing is 100% visible to your competition. Finally, the scalability of any SEO campaign is simply non-existent. If you rank one of your pages for a keyword, you can't simply insert a new keyword into what you were doing previously and rank for it, too. If you want to rank for a new keyword, you will have to start completely from scratch.

However, even with all the disadvantages, SEO is free, and if you rank well, you will attract traffic from both desktop and mobile users. This is why SEO is a perfect fit for those who have absolutely no money but do have time to spare.

**Facebook**

Facebook is to social what Google is to search. It completely dominates the world of social networks. This is why corporations, small businesses, and affiliates are present in news feeds, and some of them are making lots of money. Just like Google, Facebook offers virtually unlimited scaling capabilities. Even if you can't afford to buy advertising on Facebook, you should learn the platform because it also offers an opportunity to drive organic traffic to your offers.

Some affiliates choose to invest their time, money and other resources in building Facebook fan pages that have thousands of dedicated and engaged followers. Such pages can later be monetized through all kinds of affiliate offers. This strategy works not only for Facebook but also for Twitter and Pinterest.

When it comes to learning Facebook, there are two learning curves. The curve to learning paid advertising is similar to the one on Google. You will have to choose an audience, create ads and drive traffic. To become successful at organic sharing and community building, you need to learn to understand user behavior and to develop great content.

When it comes to user intent, Facebook also works differently than Google, but it doesn't make it any less powerful. While it's true that most people on Facebook are not looking to buy right away, the ability to start a conversation that Facebook offers is extremely powerful. We all pay much more attention to what our friends are sharing, liking and doing than we pay to the ads on the sidebar or in the middle of search results.

Being a social network, Facebook has extremely powerful targeting instruments. People share their lives on Facebook and Facebook uses this data to help advertisers deliver their message. While Instagram, Twitter, and Pinterest also have a lot of information about their users, they don't even get close to Facebook.

Facebook is becoming more and more evolved with every day. For this reason, the days of one-cent clicks are mostly over. The presence of giant corporations drives up costs across all media platforms and advertising channels, including Google and Facebook. However, Facebook does offer an opportunity for viral advertising. If you can get your target audience to share your content with their friends, your costs will most likely go down significantly.

**Display Networks and Banners**

The possibilities for display and banner advertising on the Internet are endless. Virtually all websites, including the most trusted and well-known such as Forbes and Wall Street Journal, belong to display networks. This means that you can have your ads there, especially if you are targeting a certain visitor that has been to your website before.

You will often find desktop display networks, mobile networks and those that offer both mobile and desktop advertising. Some networks are very cheap, some are expensive, and some are average-priced. They can also offer almost no targeting options at all or have some of the most advanced targeting features in the world.

With display networks, you can also run super-focused banner campaigns on just one or several specific websites of your choice. At the same time, you can target all the websites on the Internet that have, for example, 300 by 250-pixel spots available.

Display networks are one of the toughest sources of traffic to master. This is because you will not make money if you just have a great ad or if you just have a great landing page. You need a funnel, and you need all pieces of the funnel working together and delivering results. If your funnel is 95% complete, it won't work. This can be very frustrating to beginner affiliates, but that's how things often work in business. There is no difference between 0% complete and 95% complete. The only number that works is 100%. However, if you figure out how to build systems that include great banners with sufficient clicks and landing pages that convert, you can really make a lot of money.

One of the benefits that display networks offer is that they are probably the easiest to test compared to other sources of traffic. This is especially true of mobile networks because they are not so sensitive to spots below the fold. With desktop computers, you will have parts of the pages that never get clicks. The landscape is very different with mobile advertising where people tend to scroll through pages on their four, five and six-inch screens. This means that the chances of them seeing your ads on their mobile devices are much higher, even though they may be scrolling through your ads really quickly. However, if you learn to create great banners and to capture people's attention on mobile, you can succeed.

One of the issues with banner advertising is that if you want to reach scale, you will have to master advertising on websites where visitors have no or little buying intent. While you can test specific websites and categories, this is usually expensive and restrictive.

However, with banner ads and display networks you can use retargeting. Retargeting is a form of advertising where you serve ads and content to users based on their previous actions. For example, if someone visited your website where you sell computer equipment but did not buy, you can re-target them with an ad that says something similar to "Have you been looking for great offers on computer equipment? Here's what we have for you today." Because you know that a person visited your website, you know that they are interested in what you had on the website. It is just that for some reason they didn't take an action that you wanted them to take. However, knowing that a person is interested in something can be very powerful because you can include images and targeted questions in your ads that are guaranteed to attract the attention of your audience.

Display network traffic is also extremely scalable. If you make an offer work with banner and display network traffic, you'll be able to scale it almost indefinitely.

One of the problems with display network traffic is that it can become very expensive and it is the worst kind of expensive because with this kind of traffic you would be usually paying not for results such as clicks or conversions, but views. This means that you'll have to pay even if your ads do not convert. Mobile display networks are usually cheaper than mixed networks or desktop-only networks.

At the same time, display advertising offers a lot of opportunities because you are not tied to one website or one advertising account, which is what happens when you advertise on Google or Facebook. There are a lot of display networks available to you, which means that this is a golden age for this kind of opportunity. You can promote your offers on devices and in the networks that did not have the prices go up significantly because of fierce competition. This is mostly true of mobile-only and mixed networks. Some of the desktop display networks have been around for a long time and have some major players with huge budgets as members.

**Pay per view traffic**

This kind of traffic may seem confusing if you are a beginner. With pay per view or PPV traffic, you will be paying a fixed sum, usually between $0.005 and $0.002, for a popup window that is a banner or a full landing page. Usually, when a visitor to a page performs some kind of action, a third-party software prompts the browser to open a full new page or a banner.

Here's another example of how pay per view traffic may work. Let's say Jane Smith is browsing the Internet and finds a website that has five hundred wallpapers and several hundred of emoticons that she really likes.

To get these wallpapers and emoticons, Jane needs to agree to terms and conditions that include a requirement to install a toolbar that will serve ads based on her browsing history and behavior.

Because Jane needs to agree to the conditions, the software falls into the category of adware and not malware. After accepting the conditions, installing the toolbar and restarting her browser, Jane gets access to the things she was looking for. However, she will now from time to time get pop-ups when she visits certain pages or when she performs searches on Google.

The popups represent an order from PPV advertisers. From example, you can target people that visit SheepdogChurchSecurity.com. You can then specify your landing page and specify how much you are willing to pay for your landing page to show in the popup window. Now every time that Jane visits SheepdogChurchSecurity.com, a popup will show her your page. You will pay for each exposure.

This makes PPV a highly effective way of reaching an audience. PPV advertising is also very interruptive and thus hard to miss and ignore.

The most important difference between PPV advertising and typical pop-ups is the way the ads appear on the screens of the users. Typical pop-ups are generated by JavaScript, which means that they can only run on websites and devices that have JavaScript on. If the ad is shown by third-party software, which is what happens with PPV, it can show on websites that do not work with any ad networks because it's the software and not the website showing the ads. This is why with PPV you can have access to a lot of volume and a lot of targeting at the same time.

One of the biggest issues with PPV traffic is its scalability. PPV works only with desktop computers. More and more computers make it extremely hard for people to accept adware, not to mention the proliferation of mobile devices, which means that PPV market is actually shrinking.

## Native advertising

Native advertising is a relatively new form of advertising. You have probably seen them on the websites that you frequent. They look just like articles and are typically delivered by Outbrain or Taboola.

Website owners love native advertising because it produces higher click-through rates compared to other forms of advertising. This means that website owners get more revenue compared to other forms of advertising.

Affiliate marketers love native advertising because it blends in with other content seamlessly and provides an effective bridge from the website to the landing page.

Currently, native advertising is going through the stage of explosive growth. It means that you can get in while spending very little money, but with time this kind of traffic will be getting more and more expensive.

Most of the learning curve when it comes to natural advertising has to do with copywriting. If you want to use native advertising, you will need to become a copywriter who can create interesting advertorials that merge together with you native ads.

One of the issues with native ads is that users are typically in the browsing mode when they see them. Typically, native ads appear either in the middle of a page or at the bottom of a page. This means that the main intent of your audience at this point would be to spend more time reading more articles. This is why commercial conversions are harder with native ads, and click-through ratios are lower for advertorial landing pages compared to other landing pages.

Most platforms for native advertising allow you to target your audience by category or by a specific website identifier that lets your separate, say, Fox from CNN.

The scalability of your ads will depend directly on the click-through ratios of your ads. If you ads are performing well, you will have lower costs per click. If your ads are performing poorly, your costs will go through the roof, making it harder for you to scale your campaigns.

Relative costs of native ads also depend on the platforms that you will be using. If you have to deal with fixed costs per click, getting your native ads to work for you may be tough. However, if you are dealing with floating costs per click that are based on your click-through ratios, then native advertising can turn out to be quite cheap.

Finally, mobile suitability of native advertising is very good. Native advertising on mobile only is also cheaper compared to ads that run only on desktops. Such advertising can be extremely effective if you are promoting app installs or are generating leads.

**What type of traffic is best for you?**

As you can see, we've discussed a number of ways to drive traffic to your offers, but we didn't create an overall score to compare them to each other. We didn't do that because it is impossible to compare them effectively, without taking offers and target markets into consideration.

You should first focus on a market. Then decide whether you want to find something that you will be able to scale or something that will bring you quick results. Scalability often means doing more work and dealing with more challenges in order to get larger returns.

For example, the following formula can lead to massive returns: Weight loss + Facebook. If you want immediate returns, you will probably be better off if you get started with Weight Loss + PPV.

It all depends on what risks you are willing to take and what rewards interest you. Only you can figure this out.

# Putting a campaign together

So far we have covered the niches that you may want to promote. We have also discussed the ways of promoting them and talked about different types of traffic, learning curves, pros, and cons of various types of traffic.

By now you should have an idea of what you want to promote and what kind of traffic you will drive to your offers.

If you don't sign up with a few affiliate

networks. See what's trending on the major

affiliate websites such as www.ClickBank.com and www.JVZoo.com Join forums such as

Warrior Forum (free) or Stack That Money (paid).

The next step is execution and putting a campaign together.

In this section of the book, we will discuss how you can executive your campaigns. We will be talking about landing pages, angles to approach your selling and conversions.

Simply choosing a vertical and a way to drive your traffic is not enough. You also need to figure out how to effectively sell to you audience and how to great an ROI that will work for you.

Once you are ready to promote your offer and get your affiliate link, you have two choices. You can either direct-link to your offers or send traffic to a landing page.

Direct-linking may work if you already have a list and have a relationship with the list. If you don't, then simply dropping your affiliate links and sending traffic straight to the offer adds zero value, because you are not doing anything that the merchant couldn't do on its own.

This is why if you don't have a list, you probably won't be able to make money by simply providing people with a direct affiliate link. It is possible to make money this way by buying advertising and driving traffic straight to the merchant, but such cases are extremely rare. One of the issues, why it's really hard to make money this way, is that the barrier to entry is non-existent. If making money were so easy, everybody would be doing it. If you had an ad that was driving traffic directly to an offer, anyone could copy your ad, get his or her own link and start making money.

This is why most affiliates use landing pages and funnels to add value to what they are promoting.

For example, if a prospect is looking to buy a weight-loss program and stumbles upon a page with some radical claims and a button to buy now, he or she will probably not buy right away. The prospect will need more information about the product. He or she will feel compelled to do some research, gather facts, read testimonials and reviews. This would often mean navigating away from the sales page, going to Google and researching the product or the competition further.

After carrying this research, the prospect is more likely to buy. At the same time, the prospect may decide against purchasing the product that captured his or her interest in the first place. However, he or she may decide on a different product and use someone else's affiliate link to buy it.

This is why one of the great opportunities for affiliate marketers is to insert themselves into the research and buying process and provide suggestions for making a decision when it comes to certain products or services. This is also why you will see a lot of landing pages that offer reviews of multiple products or look like FAQ created by the guy next door.

However, if you pay attention to those FAQs, you will see that they are not really answers to frequently asked questions. They are answers to concerns and barriers that prevents prospects from buying.

When creating a landing page, don't get stuck in technical details. Start with thinking about what the visitor needs to know in order to take the action that you want him or her to take. Then think about what is preventing the visitors from taking that action, what concerns and issues they may have that will stop them from doing what you want them to do.

Next, give them positive reasons and at the same time show to them why the negatives that they believe about your product or service are not true.

For example, when it comes to a lot of products in the weight-loss niche, your prospects will have the following questions:

- Does the product work?

- Will the product work for me?

- Is it safe?

- What is the success rate of this product?

- How much work will it take to make the product work?

- Is this the best deal I can find?

If all your merchant has is a page with a buy now button and the prospect doesn't buy, these are the question that he or she would have. These are the questions that the prospect needs answered before he or she buys.

This is why you want to answer these questions as best as you can. These are several ways how you can do this. You can create your landing page depending on the method that you want to use.

The first method is to create a landing page that looks like a blog. The second one is to create a news-y looking article. In the article, you can explain what the product is, what it does, why it is so successful and why the prospect needs to order the product today. Such articles typically use "news" style templates, and the pages look similar to what a user would see on Fox, CNN or CNBC. Some affiliates also create pages that incorporate latest weather forecasts using a geoscript and widgets that show real-time news. All of this makes prospects think that they are reading a story that deserves coverage from major news sources.

Another way to go with a landing page is to create a classic advertorial. Advertorials look like articles, have testimonials and often add scarcity at the end.

Now let's discuss typical mistakes that affiliates make when promoting their offers.

The first mistake is the confusion of where the audience is in the buying process. It's one thing if your traffic is ready to buy. Selling to people who have made up their minds about buying is really easy. However, it may also turn out that your traffic is not seeking the solution that you are offering. In this case, one of the tasks of your landing page is to explain the problem and possibly change the opinion about what you have to offer.

The second mistake is creating inconsistent funnels. For example, some affiliate promoting dating offers would create landing pages that promise "100% FREE ACCESS FOREVER."

When a visitor clicks on the link, he or she ends up on a dating site where he or she needs to pay for everything. The visitor realizes that the promise was false, gets confused, goes away and never returns.

Several weeks later the merchant realizes that the traffic from the affiliate doesn't convert into paid subscribers, kicks out the affiliate and the affiliate decides that "affiliate marketing doesn't work."

While this scenario may sound ridiculous, this is what happens in the affiliate marketing world every day. Affiliates get so excited about promoting a product or a service that they forget what they are promoting in the first place.

They use banners that promise one thing. The banners lead to landing pages with a different promise, and when the visitor finally gets to the merchant page, the final offer is completely different from what the visitor saw during the previous steps.

As an affiliate, you want to be very consistent with your funnels. From the ads, to the landing pages, to the offers, the message should be consistent everywhere.

Choosing your message should go side-by-side with choosing your marketing angle. You want to have a deep understanding of who your offer is for and what specific benefits it contains.

To find this information, start with emailing your affiliate manager. Ask for background information. Find how the offer was created and the story behind it. Talk to the merchant about the advertising that works best for the offer and the profile of an ideal customer.

One of the best things you can do is see who else is promoting the offer and sign up for the offer as a customer.

You also want to study your merchant's competition. Who else is selling something similar to the same target audience? What are they doing in the same manner? What are they doing differently and why?

Finally, you want to study your competition, meaning other affiliates. Are there any direct rivals that are promoting the same offer? What do you see when you search for the offer on Google? What angles are other affiliates using? You want to pay special attention to the affiliates that are getting the most exposure and are spending the most money. If they are doing it for quite some time, it means that what they are doing is working. Their budgets simply wouldn't last long if they were losing money on

the offer and the campaigns.

Once you find out the answers to the questions above and study the offer, the market, and the competition, you should get a pretty good picture of what is working and what is not working.

One of the best ways to make quick progress is to not invent something radically new, but take something that is working and apply it to what you are doing. Once you establish the most popular angles for your offer, simply copy them and use them. You can come up with new angles and test them against old angles later. You do not need a lot of new ideas to get started. Simply see what everybody is doing and copy things that are working. It is simply impossible to compare different campaigns if you don't benchmark first the campaigns that are already out there. Once you do have some numbers to work with. You can try and improve them. Trying to improve something that may not be working in the first place is a big and costly mistake.

When coming up with the angles and marketing messages for your offers, mix and match various demographics, desires, and needs.

Here are some of the questions that should be helpful:

- Who is the target customer?

- What does the offer provide to the target audience?

- In what way does it do it?

- Why is it important to the audience?

For example, if you are working on promoting a dating offer, you can segment the market in the following ways:

- Singles

- Divorcees

- People seeing short-term affairs

- Desperate virgins

- People new to the area

- Serial daters

Depending on the target audience, the offer may provide a number of different benefits:

- Meeting new people

- Meeting like-minded people

- Going on dates

- Having online conversations

- Getting attention

- Finding friends

- Finding romantic partners

- Getting invites to events

And so on.

As you can see, with all the options available to you, it simply would make no sense to try and promote all the angles at the same time. It is impossible to be all things to all people. This is why it is so important to choose the right angle and promote your offers to the right audience.

# Practical tips

### Introduction to practical tips

With the tips, questions, and suggestions from the previous parts of this book, you should have enough material to get started with your landing page, campaigns, messages and marketing angles.

One of the parts of your message that you absolutely need to master is the call to action.

A lot of affiliate marketers complain that they don't get the results that they want from their traffic and blame the traffic for it. However, if you look at their landing pages and offers, you would often see lack of clarity. Do people that end up on your pages clearly, really, completely understand what they are getting and what they need to do to get your product or service? This may seem like an obvious question. However, if you examine ten or twenty different affiliate landing pages, you will see a lot of problems. Too often affiliate marketers are taking for granted things that should not be taking for granted. They also make assumptions about their visitors that are simply not true and have no basis in real life.

Most people do a good job of following instructions. Following instructions is something we've been told to do since we were little. For the most part, kids follow the instructions that they get from their teachers. Adults stop on red, go on green, stay in lanes they are supposed to stay in, fill out the paperwork they need to fill out and so on. Most people are conditioned from infancy to follow instructions when they see them.

A lot of affiliate marketers often forget about it. They leave too much for people to figure out, ignoring the fact that confused or uncertain visitors will not try to figure things out. They will simply leave the page and go elsewhere.

If you were to examine landing pages, banners and even offline marketing materials and environments such as restaurant menus, in-store signage and media ads, you will see plenty of assumptions that marketers make about their target audience. These assumptions usually leave plenty of room for confusion and lack of action. For example, a restaurant may have a menu in Italian without a description in English. A store may have signage that describes departments but doesn't say whether the departments offer men's or women's clothing. When you put together any part of your funnel, any part of a marketing campaign or a landing page, you should always carefully examine them for the presumption of knowledge or beliefs on the part of the visitor, prospect or customer. It is much better to give very extensive instructions than to have a lack of clarity.

It is also important to remember that people get anxious every time they don't know what to expect as a next step. This is why you always want to give instructions about what is going to happen after people take the step that you want them to take.

As an affiliate marketer, you may not care about what happens after you deliver a lead or a sign-up to your merchant and this may cause you to ignore talking about this to the visitors of your landing page. However, the question about what is going to happen next is most likely extremely important to your visitors and ignoring it may be a mistake.

Make sure that you have multiple calls to action on your page that ask people to do what you want them to do. Never assume that the audience will figure it out on its own and act in the way you want it to act.

Without a doubt, you've seen calls to action on websites multiple times. The simplest call to action is "CLICK HERE."

You can also use a variety of other calls to action that clearly explain to the visitors what you want them to do next, for example

Download Now

Get Instant Access Now

Sign Up Now

Sign Up For Immediate Access

Download The App Here

And so on

## Practical tips for landing pages

Creation of landing pages is often more complex than the creation of a Google Ad or a Facebook ad. One of the best ways to get started with landing pages is to get the same templates that your competitors are using to promote their affiliate offers. Once you install a template, become comfortable with it. Learn how to change the headlines, images and lists.

All of this is very easy to accomplish. Edit the copy, change the tracking links, upload your own files. This is how you can create a landing page in twenty to thirty minutes.

To create really good landing pages, you will need to get a basic understanding of HTML and CSS. Many pages also use JavaScript, although you do not need to learn Java to be able to use tools based on JavaScript.

JavaScript snippets can be very powerful. With their help, you can display today's date as the expiration date, display tomorrow's date, display a countdown timer, fill in the location of a user and so on.

The good news is that you don't need to understand the code. Once you find the tools that you need, you can simply insert them into landing pages by copying and pasting the code.

Whenever you see a landing page that you think is worthy of attention, click on "Save As..." and save it. Also, make a few screenshots, so that you would always be able to see how the page looked in case it goes down or the code in your saved files gets altered.

With time you will be able to create landing pages of your own, but in the beginning learning to modify what works should get your started and allow you to test and try various things.

One of the areas we haven't discussed in detail is copywriting itself. While it is true that you can make money with poor banners, poor ad copy, and poor landing page copy, such instances are becoming more and more rare.

While copywriting is one of the really great skills to have and develop, you can start with riding off the back of the affiliates that have already mastered that skill and are making money.

**How to Optimize Campaigns**

Campaign optimization is what separates amateur affiliates from those who make serious money in this business. No matter how skilled you are, the majority of campaigns that you launch will fail. Some will fail miserably. Some of the best affiliate marketers in the world say that 80% to 90% of their campaigns fail.

Your goal, therefore, should not be to try and improve these numbers. Your goal should be to separate winners from losers and quickly and efficiently as possible. You also shouldn't be getting emotional about your numbers. Affiliate marketing is all about finding those 1 out of 10 or 2 out of 10 campaigns that are going to be winners, scaling them and making a lot of money with them, so that in the future you could test quickly and get rid of 8 out of 10 or 9 out of 10 losers that you will have. In affiliate marketing, failure has a strong correlation to success, which is why if you want to create campaigns that make a lot of money, you will also create campaigns that are losers.

What separates successful affiliates from those who fail is the optimization philosophy. Successful affiliates quickly identify losers and also pay attention to the campaigns that contain opportunities so that they can extract money from them and scale them.

In order to be able to do this, you need to become focused and to learn to shut off all the distractions.

Let's assume that you have chosen an affiliate offer, have created a Facebook campaign and are driving traffic to a landing page. In order to be able to track your results, you need to install tracking software from the very beginning.

Such a software can help you uncover insights that tell you in what cities and areas your offer converts, what time of the day works best for your conversions, which landing pages, headlines, and layouts are more effective, which ads convert better and more.

If you don't have access to the information that can help you answer these questions, you are blindly relying on luck, and that usually doesn't work.

There are a number of platforms and analytics tools that can help affiliates track their campaigns.

If you are just getting started, you can use free tools such as Facebook pixel or Google Analytics.

Facebook pixel allows you to install several lines of code on your pages and track conversions, build and analyze audiences and learn about how visitors use your website. With Facebook pixel, you can also create various events, use ad tracking and optimize your campaigns in various ways.

Google Analytics is a free service from Google that tracks website visitors and reports data about the visitors and the visits, such as visit durations, bounce rate, most popular pages on the website and so on. If you integrate Google Analytics with Google Adwords, you'll be able to track your conversions, the quality of your landing pages and much more.

If you have multiple campaigns running on different platforms, you may want to use other tools, many of which have both free and paid versions.

One of the most popular tools that affiliates use to track and measure conversions across multiple platforms is Tracking202 or T202. This platform is self-hosted and extremely customizable. It has most of the data points that you will need to make better decisions about your campaigns. However, this platform can be hard to figure out, and if you are just getting started with affiliate marketing, you probably want something easier.

CPV Lab is a self-hosted platform that allows you to track everything from direct links to campaign funnels and lead paths.

Voluum is a platform that has both free and paid packages. It is hosted in the cloud, so you don't have to worry about installing it or keeping it up to date or up to the volume of your traffic.

Thrive is a tracking platform that competes with Voluum. It has a lot of great reviews and a lot of features.

The main goals of using tracking software are to know when your campaigns are profitable and when they are not and to get insights from the traffic that visits your pages, funnels, and paths.

To maximize the profitability of your campaigns, you need to be testing everything constantly. Try different offers, different angles, various types of landing pages and ads. When working with landing pages, try different headlines, testimonials vs. no testimonials, different pictures and images and so on.

The most important thing to test is the offer itself. Once you find a winning offer, test different versions of it and test them on different networks. For example, if you are promoting dating websites and Match.com is beating eHarmony.com, as your next step test Match.com on Affiliate Network A versus Match.com on Affiliate Network B versus Match.com on Affiliate Network C.

Such testing is extremely important because the same offer can be performing very differently on different networks. If you find an offer that works, test it on various networks and see if you can beat your current numbers. Your goal should be to find the network where the offer will convert best. Once you find the best network for the best offer, try to beat your numbers by experimenting with different marketing angles. Successful affiliate marketers would usually try at least five different angles. When creating new angles, you will need to tweak both your ads and the landing pages to make them consistent with the approach that you are using.

A lot of affiliate marketers get lazy and only tweak the ads, but not the landing pages because it is much faster and easier to tweak an ad than to tweak a landing page. This is why they will use a system like the following:

Marketing Angle 1: Ads 1, 2, 3 – Landing Page A – Offer 1

Marketing Angle 2: Ads 3, 4, 5 – Landing Page A – Offer 1

Marketing Angle 3: Ads 6, 7, 8 – Landing Page A – Offer 1

Marketing Angle 4: Ads 9, 10, 11 – Landing Page A – Offer 1

Marketing Angle 5: Ads 12, 13 – Landing Page A – Offer 1

Instead of doing the work to maximize the effectiveness of the funnel and having it look like this:

Marketing Angle 1: Ads 1, 2, 3 – Landing Page A – Offer 1

Marketing Angle 2: Ads 3, 4, 5 – Landing Page B – Offer 1

Marketing Angle 3: Ads 6, 7, 8 – Landing Page C – Offer 1

Marketing Angle 4: Ads 9, 10, 11 – Landing Page D – Offer 1

Marketing Angle 5: Ads 12, 13 – Landing Page E – Offer 1

In most cases, your conversions will be higher if you do tweak the landing pages and create a separate page for every angle.

Another important reason to do all the testing is banner blindness. Banner blindness is what happens when you run the same ads for the same audience for a period of time. This period may be weeks, months or, in the worst-case scenario, days. You will see your conversions going down because your audience is used to your ads and doesn't notice them. When this happens, the number of clicks that you get will go down. The reduction of the number of clicks usually leads to increased ad costs and lower margins. For your campaigns to be effective in long-term, you can't have razor-thin margins. The solution to this problem is to constantly test new ads, landing pages and images. This will allow you not only to improve your conversions, but also to keep your ads and landing pages fresh and new-looking, which is very important when you have competition.

Earlier in the book we talked about the fact that the easiest way to get started with affiliate marketing is to take a look at what other affiliates are doing and create something similar.

If you do get started and become at least somewhat successful, others will start copying you. There is nothing you can do about this.

The only answer to this problem is the answer that Ray Kroc, the founder of McDonald's franchise, gave when he was asked if he was afraid of the competition. His answer was the following: "We invent faster than they copy us." If you take a look at McDonald's and its competition today, over fifty years later, you will see that the formula is still working for McDonald's. They are able to remain very successful because they invent faster than the competition. This is also what you have to do if you want to stay on top of your game in the field of affiliate marketing.

One of the toughest skills that you will need to master as an affiliate marketer is the ability to tell when you need to stop.

For example, an affiliate marketer would run a campaign and get an ROI of negative 75%. He or she would then optimize the campaign and bring the ROI to negative 50%. On the one hand, optimization did improve the results. On the other hand, the marketer is still losing money.

Before it was a loss of $150 on $200. After it is a loss of $100 on $200.

The question then becomes: at what point do you stop working on a campaign that is losing money, label it as a loser and move on?

The answer is simple. If you are running an offer that should be converting and your ten best marketing angles do not get you a loss of less than 50%, then there's no point to optimize ads or copy on the landing page.

If your best efforts lead to abysmal results, there is no point to try to improve the results. Sure, you can spend weeks and months optimizing a campaign and maybe turn a loser into a winner, but it is much easier to find winners and win with them than to try and turn losers into winners.

Marketing angles are the best indicator of whether you are on the right track. If you are getting wide fluctuations on your results depending on your angles, it means that you are close to a breakthrough. If, however, all of your angles deliver equally abysmal results and it looks like you'll have to spend weeks optimizing the campaigns to get to a positive ROI, then it's the time to cut the losses and move on.

If all angles lead to similar losses, there is something wrong either with the offer, with the traffic sources or with your calculations. You can't change any of these by writing better headlines or better copy. The best thing you can do in this scenario is get out and move to a better offer.

## Stats to Live By

Some of the most important numbers that you should be paying attention to are the following

## Earnings per click or EPC

This number is equal to the amount of money that you are making divided by the number of clicks that you need to get to obtain a conversion. If, for example, Offer 1 has EPC of $1 and Offer 2 has EPC of 90c and your costs are the same, then Offer 1 is more profitable than Offer 2.

EPC is always more important than the payout.

It may seem that an offer that pays $100 is better than an offer that pays $5, but it is the EPC number that shows how much money you are making, not just the payout number.

Don't allow merchants to seduce you with seemingly high payout numbers. Always look at the EPC.

**Cost per Click or CPC**

This number can either be a direct cost if you are buying clicks to a website on a platform like

Google Adwords or Facebook or it can be an inferred cost if you pay for views and not clicks. In this latter case, you can divide the amount you are paying by the number of clicks to get the CPC. For example, let's say you paid $2 for 1000 views. Out of 1000 views, you got 5 clicks. To get your CPC, divide $2 by 5 clicks. Your CPC is 40 cents per click.

Generally speaking, traffic sources that change per click are easier to track than traffic sources where you pay per view or per action. Such traffic sources are also less vulnerable to banner blindness, but often they offer less flexibility than display networks and other sources of traffic where you would pay based on the number of views.

**Cost per 1000 impressions or CPM**

This rate varies significantly depending on a traffic source. When you know your numbers, you can test different strategies and approaches. For example, you can lower your CPM trying to reduce your CPC, or you can increase your CPM and see if you get higher-quality views that will lead to more clicks.

**Earnings per View or EPV**

This stat is similar to Earnings Per Click. It tracks users that saw your landing page but did not take advantage of your offer.

**Cost per View or CPV**

If you are buying traffic on a per-view basis, then knowing this number and comparing it to your EPV will show you how far you are from being profitable.

For example, if you are bidding on views and are paying twenty cents per view, but are getting EPV of thirty cents per view, you have 50% positive ROI.

**Click through Rate or CTR**

CTR is an important number for both your ads and your landing pages. If you spend any times on the affiliate forums, you will find a lot of people trying to compare their CTRs. What you need to know is that there is no such thing as a typical CTR. The clicks that you are getting from your ads or from your landing pages can only be compared to similar ads and landing pages. There is simply no point in comparing an ad created to attract as many clicks as possible to an ad designed only for users who have strong buying intent. Similarly, comparing a CTR for a banner with a fake virus alert to a CTR for a long-form sales letter is completely useless.

There are a lot of things you can do to increase CTRs of various standalone pieces, but what matters, in the end, is the conversion rate of the entire funnel.

The best affiliates work hard to improve their CTRs without sacrificing visitor quality. This skill is hard to learn but very useful to have.

**Conversion Rate**

Just like it makes no sense to compare different CTRs, it makes no sense to compare different conversion rates. You do not need to have the best conversion rate in the industry to be successful and to be making a lot of money. For example, a low conversion rate and a high CTR can work just fine if you are using traffic from CPM sources. A low conversion rate can also work just fine if you are driving high-quality, expensive traffic.

While you would always benefit from an improved conversion rate, there are many ways to strike a profit in affiliate marketing.

# Conclusion

Thank you for reading this book. I hope you have gained quite a few insights from reading it. We have tried to bring you some of the most complicated concepts using simple and easy to understand language. This being said, a lot of things in the affiliate marketing will only become clear to you once you get some first-hand experience. Choose a few offers, run a few campaigns, get your feet wet.

All the best and good luck!

# A to Z Affiliate Checklist

Preparation stage

1.   Decide on the niche. What market will you focus on?

2.   Decide what traffic sources you will be using. Where will you be buying traffic?

3.   Decide on the intent of your leads. What strategy will you choose?

4.   Decide on your ad placements. Where will you run your ads? What ads will you create?

5.   Is there an alignment between your ads and the quality of your leads? If not, how can you improve the alignment?

6.  Research your best-performing

competition.

Use spy tools such as SpyFu to find top five

advertisers in your market. Study what they are

doing, including the offers, marketing

messages and angles, price points and types of

landing pages

7.  Get access to at least one of the offers that

you have discovered in the previous step

8.  Contact affiliate managers and find as

much as possible about the offers

9.  Re-read sections of this book that describe

your market and your offers

10.  Contact your rep at the traffic source and

discuss with them your market and your offer

Creation stage

1.   Develop at least five marketing angles for your offer. Use information you collected in the preparation stage to draft different marketing angles. Make sure to include the ones that you learned about from your competition.

2.   Create a landing page for Marketing Angle 1. Do so by editing or re-creating a page that is already successful. Verify that the copy matches the angle and that ads and your landing page are consistent and congruent

3.   Create three variations for Marketing Angle 1. Come up with new headlines, images, re-write the copy.

4.   Repeat steps 1-3 for remaining marketing angles

5.   Choose and set up tracking software.

6. Decide what you will do with traffic that is unsuitable for your purposes such as traffic from other countries or devices that you are not targeting.

7. Upload your ads to the ad platforms

8. Finalize campaign settings

9. Double check campaign settings

10. Plan to give some time for the campaign to be approved

11. Collect initial campaign performance data

Optimization stage

1. Perform full review of your campaigns. What ROI are you getting? Are you spending less, more or exactly as much as you expected to spend? Does the campaign has a potential to

meet your revenue targets? If not, go to autopsy phase

2.   Assess your offers. Do you have a clear winner? What is the conversion rate for different offers? Are there definite losers? If yes, remove them.

3.   Assess your marketing angles. Do some angles perform better than others? Are there clear winners? What are the conversion rates? Are there definite losers? If yes, make a note and remove them.

4.   Assess your ads. Calculate the conversions, establish the winners. Remove the losers.

5.   Based on the results of your optimization efforts decide on your next steps.

Order of priorities to consider:

1.  Figure out which offer is performing best

2.  Figure out the best-performing marketing angles

3.  Test the best-performing angles with different kinds of landing pages

4.  Identify the ads that perform the best

5.  Think about what makes them perform and create new ads trying to beat the current best-performing ads

6.  Try different targeting options and restriction options such as times when you run your ads.


Ongoing priorities:

1.  Remove worst-performing ads

2.  Create a list of placements that are working

for you

7.  Collect more data. Let campaigns run some

more. Get the results.

Continue optimization efforts until you reach

one of two conclusions:

1.  The campaign is producing satisfactory

results. Move to campaign maintenance stage.

2.  The campaign is failing. Move to the

autopsy stage.

Campaign Maintenance Stage

1.  Calculate your ROI. Are you hitting your targets?

2.  Spend some time on prevention. What is likely to degrade as time passes by?

1.  Blacklist placements that do not perform well

2.  Create new ads to avoid banner blindness

3.  Test new variations of landing pages

3. Run the campaigns more. Collect even more data

4. Assess the results. Is the campaign still performing well?

5. Try to scale the campaign

Autopsy stage

1.  Record all the numbers and steps that you've taken. Make notes about marketing angles, <u>offers,</u> landing pages, ads, placements and your target audience. Keep a written record of everything

2.  Review the campaign. Identify the factors that were responsible for campaign failure.

3.  Think about future opportunities and steps. What did you learn from running this campaign? Would it be possible to run the campaign profitably in the future?

4.  Create a swipe file for future reference.

# BEFORE YOU GO

## If you liked this book you may like these other books from Mark Thomas

## Check out more books by Mark Thomas

# Free Bonus

As Promised Here Is Your Guide To
Creating More Hours In Your Day:
Discover How To Fit 48 Hours Of Work
In A Day

GET YOUR FREE COPY

# LEARN HOW TO GET MORE DONE IN A DAY

Do you feel stuck, stressed, and pissed because you aren't able to get all of your most important tasks done in a day? Perhaps this book can be the answer to your struggles. Learn the ways to manage your time to get more things done in a day and free up time do things you enjoy in life. Procrastination and Distractions are the biggest enemy of time management. This book will teach you the exact strategies to conquer procrastination.

Download "The Clockwork Course" For FREE

# If You Want Free Best Selling Kindle Books Delivered Straight To Your Inbox

## JOIN OUR FREE KINDLE BOOK CLUB!

## BE PART OF THE CLUB

# Introduction: What you need to know about Airbnb

## Airbnb Description and Features

Airbnb is an online marketplace website that allows its users to list, find and rent homes from other Airbnb users. You can list regular apartments and homes. You can also become creative with what you list. For example, one of the accommodations listed on Airbnb in NYC in 2016 was a taxi minivan parked on one of the streets of Long Island City.

You can set your availability calendar and charge what you want for your accommodation. Obviously, you are not going to be the only Airbnb host, and you will have competition, so your pricing needs to be reasonable. However, it is a marketplace and just like in every other marketplace there are different price points and different kinds of renters and hosts.

The idea of renting space is not new. However, Airbnb and similar platforms bring a new level of convenience, speed, and transparency to it.

Why do most people rent their homes on Airbnb?

According to a study Airbnb conducted in San Francisco, the average Airbnb guest visits the city for 5.5 days and spends $1,045.

56% of the hosts said that they use Airbnb to cover mortgage or rent costs while 42% of hosts use the platform to pay for everyday living expenses.

**The History Of Airbnb**

As of February of 2016, Airbnb had over 60 million users. The website is active in over 192 countries, 57,000 cities and has over 500 thousand stays per night.

Airbnb was created in San Francisco in August 2008. At the time, Airbnb founders Brian Chesky, and Joe Gebbia couldn't afford the rent for their apartment in San Francisco, and so they started renting out their living room as a bed and breakfast kind of accommodation. The room could fit three guests who used air mattresses.

In February of 2008, Airbnb's third co-founder, technical architect Nathan Blecharczyk, joined Chesky and Gebbia. In the initial stages, the founders targeted high-profile events with a shortage of lodging.

To come up with the funding for the project, the co-founders created special editions of breakfast cereals. The cereals included "Obama O's" and "Cap'n McCains," named after presidential candidates Barack Obama and John McCain. In just two months, Chesky, Blecharczyk, and Gebbia sold 800 boxes of their cereals at $40 per box, raising over $30,000.

In January of 2009, Airbnb became a part of Y Combinator's winter session that consisted of three months of training. Airbnb co-founders used the $20,000 investment they received from Y Combinator to visit New York and meet with NYC's users.

However, the company kept growing exponentially. In February of 2011, Airbnb celebrated 1 million bookings since its opening in August 2008. A little less than in a year, in January of 2012, Airbnb announced that 5 million bookings had been made through the platform. Then, in another five months, the company had 10 million nights booked. Of these bookings, 75% happened outside of the continental US.

**A brief overview of requirements and things to consider when becoming an Airbnb host**

To become an Airbnb host, you need to be at least 18 years old. If you plan to rent your bedroom and sleep on a couch, you need to make sure that you are willing to accept the lifestyle changes that will come with this arrangement.

Also, cleanliness is extremely important. For example, you can't have dirty laundry on the floor or your things in a mess all over the apartment. This will not be okay with your guests.

You need to be very clear and upfront about the pricing, amenities, your building, neighborhood, and expectations.

While it's not a requirement, you do want to consider investing in additional linens and towels for your guests.

On Airbnb calendar, you can block dates when your apartment is not available so that you can spend time by yourself or with your family. To keep the experience of your prospective guests positive you need to maintain an accurate calendar at all times.

When renting an entire space such as a home, apartment or a boat where you won't be on site during the stay of your guests, you need to make sure that the accommodation is prepared before a check-in, that guests can get help during check-ins and their stay at your rental and that a check-out can be performed properly.

Renting your property is a business. It may be a small scale business for you, but it's still a business.

Just like any other business, this business is not for everyone. If you are very picky about how things should be in your apartment or if you are easily annoyed by other people's habits, then this business may not be for you.

**Additional details**

**Check with your local authorities if you are legally allowed to rent your place through Airbnb.**

Airbnb is a marketplace that facilitates transactions. A transaction doesn't happen between you and Airbnb. It happens between you and your guests. It is your responsibility to make sure that such transactions are legal in your municipality.

New York City, for example, prohibits rentals of full apartments for less than 30 days. At the end of 2015, Airbnb released internal data confirming that the majority of NYC Airbnb rentals violated New York's short-term leasing laws.

In June of 2016, the New York State Senate voted to approve a bill that prohibited online advertising of short-term rentals of full apartments. The measure made it illegal to rent an entire apartment on Airbnb or any of its competitors' websites.

San Francisco legalized short-term rentals in the city on February 1, 2015. However, the law allows for rentals where a host is not present to last a maximum of 90 days a year. Violators are subject to a fine of $484 per day for first-time offenders and $968 for repeat offenders. In addition to this, hosts are required to register and apply for a permit from the Office of Short Term Rental. The fee to register is $50 for every two years. Hosts also need to apply for a business license and have liability insurance.

**Check your lease to make sure that you are allowed to sublet.** Even if you own your home, verify that you are not violating any homeowners' association rules.

**While having furniture is not a requirement for listing a space on Airbnb, having an unfurnished accommodation will severely restrict the amount of guests that will be interested in staying at your rental.**

## Check out more books by Mark Thomas

Thank you again for downloading this book!

If you enjoyed this book, then I'd like to ask you for a favor, would you be kind enough to leave a review for this book on Amazon? It'd be greatly appreciated!

Thank you and good luck! ☺

-Mark Thomas

www.ingramcontent.com/pod-product-compliance
Lightning Source LLC
Chambersburg PA
CBHW071759200526
45167CB00017B/520